Peace they didn't extend

Acknella Ndoro

Acknella Ndoro /IngramSpark
Toronto, Ontario. Canada
www.themeadowofhope.com

Publisher's Note: This is a work of fiction. Names, characters, places, and incidents are a product of the author's imagination. Locales and public names are sometimes used for atmospheric purposes. Any resemblance to actual people, living or dead, or to businesses, companies, events, institutions, or locales is completely coincidental.

Book Layout © 2020 BookDesignTemplates.com

Peace they didn't extend/ Acknella Ndoro.
ISBN 978-1-7771142-0-6

CONTENTS

Darkness comforts me

Heart torn apart,

They used a grenade for it

My spirit,

They sucked into a blackhole,

My soul cries to go home

But, alas,

I am stuck on this rock I call home

The distant sirens awake me from the slumber

So annoying to be distanced

Distanced from the sweet nightmares

Please, don't wake me up

Darkness comforts me.

I have told my legs to sleep all day,

Eyes swollen; tear ducts can't produce any more

Rubbery arms and legs,

Sweating in the middle of winter,

Thy trauma is a heater

Curtains drawn,

Time stood still when the bomb dropped

So callous,

So dark the heart of men

But don't disturb me

Darkness comforts me.

I seek total quietness,

I think deep space has it

I seek solitude,

My mother's womb was it

I am a ring of Uranus,

Surrounded but separated

Broken, crushed and hollow,

Please, don't bother me

As I seek a place far, far away

Humanity can't invade my special space

It's a cave I dive into

I am throwing shade to light

Because darkness comforts me.

Gun is better for the arrow

Phone rings and no one picks it up

We are all catatonic

A premonition of the heavy nuclear warhead

Whistling towards my abode

The cycle ends and it rings again

One of us stands up and goes to answer it

They speak for seconds, turn around

And send deep, poisonous arrows

Into my family's hearts

I knew then as I know now

Gun is better for the arrow.

Sire, the head, had chosen to bid farewell

Farewell to this wretched world

He went to surrender his life on a tree

I haven't seen the tree

But I want to think that it was a sycamore tree

He drained the life in him

And never came back to say goodbye

What happened?

Who said what to him?

Surely a troubled soul he was

A trooper, a fighter for all that life called unto him

Now surrendering to the picket wires of the Hades

Oh, father!

Gun is better for the arrow.

He is gone, a family tragedy

The pain of the arrow in my chest

The arrow from that nuclear warhead

Left a burning hole on my heart

Too deep

Too wide

No surgeon can make the seams meet

I am wandering through life

Catching a glance

Squinting my eyes to the horrors before me

Understanding why the surrender came

Yet knowing

That the race must be finished

I was hurt and I am hurting

He was my first love

So, I ask again

Wouldn't the gun have been better for the arrow?

<u>**Breathe**</u>

I want to cry

But this is not the right place

I want to curl into foetus position

But my mommy's tummy is not here

Not here for comfort

I want to run

Run to the far end of the world

But I have a feeling

That life will find me over there.

The darkness that surrounds me

Has become a shroud

The silence I long for

Is too noisy

The love I crave

Has been anything

But a road made of jagged saw

I am bleeding

I want to breathe

My very last

But life won't take me.

How do you run from yourself?

I am sick and tired of me

Wherever I go,

There I am

If I hide my shadow

Would I find a cave for my soul?

How do you live with yourself?

I am suffocating me

There is no second to breathe

It's intense

It's crazy

And I am part of it

I need that release

So that at long last

I can learn

Learn to breathe again.

Meaning of life

Born in a world full of suffering

No one told me who to choose as parents

They didn't tell me which country

Which country of the world to be born into

I am not even sure who they are

All I remember is starting to know life

Life on earth as a child

Who are my parents?

How did they qualify to be mine?

Why was I born?

What is the meaning of my life?

I got to be who I am

With questions guiding me

I am still trying to figure me out

Do you know you?

There is suffering in this world

Some suffering we bring to ourselves

But not all, right?

Is it true that we have a choice?

A choice over everything?

It's a dark world,

Wars are happening right now

There are children sleeping hungry

Hungry on the streets right now

People losing their loved ones

People losing jobs right now

There are polluted,

Evil politicians everywhere

But there is that small group

A luck few that are winning

The question is,

Which category are you in right now?

Life so unfair, so unforgiving

Life so beautiful, yet so ugly

Far away in my soul a cry

A cry upsurges into a crescendo to hold on

What am I holding onto?

I really don't know

Hope so feeble

Yet not so easily broken

I am holding on to mine

I don't know the meaning of life

I don't know why I am who I am

I stand to guard for hope

Because without it,

I will not get up in the morning

I am holding on

With the belief that one day

One day I will know

The meaning of my life.

<u>Crocodile skin</u>

They rejected her but they love her

The scale tipped over to rejection

They say they are sorry

Yet, they don't mean it

She used to cry but not anymore

The crocodile tears take form of their own now

Her skin hardened,

Scales so thick like dry tar

Hardened to the water of the universe

So that she can swim

Swim in the shark infested territories.

Crushed spirit, broken heart

Dreamily, she pictures a past life

So long ago,

With the sands of Egypt in rear

There she was a woman

A woman with a heart

Normal, clueless to the wickedness

Wickedness of her species

They played countless evil games

Until she shed her humanity

The present skin shows a coarse diamond

A bejewelled spirit

She wears the skin of a crocodile.

Sailing without wind

Sick, twisted, vile world

Apocalyptic yet not so dark and out

Smithereens of what life was all about

Little gaps and glimpses

Glimpses of the perfect world

A picture can't say a thousand words,

They are aiming for the heart,

Aiming for my mind

The epicentre of my world

But you will not prevail

I am sailing without wind,

But I will make it.

He is here to shoot

Don't shoot to kill

I am here for the goal

I am here by the grace

You will not venture far and wide

I will box in the matters of my soul

Try, try and try again

But you hold the wrong tackle

You don't know me

Because you didn't make me

You wish that I was anchored

Anchored to the haven

But I will sail the river of life,

Even without wind.

Pursuit of happiness

Life so unfair,

So unfeeling,

I know of what I carry,

A heavy-load, a trailer truck wouldn't pick up

Years of pain, sorrow and torture being thrown my way,

What did I do to deserve it?

I wonder when will my breakthrough be here?

Please don't be quiet on me,

Don't sit there and tell me that what my life has given so far

Is all there is.

Where is my happiness?

Smiling is starting to hurt my mouth

Because it's not coming from deep within

But from somewhere on the surface,

Tears roll down my face and I will not be wiping them away

My heart is broken,

A thousand little pieces are floating in my chest

Little remnants of a blown galaxy

Because I have pursued happiness and not found it.

23

Who gets to decide, how much of one's pain is enough?

Is there a letter-box in hell?

No! No! Please make it a telegram,

An emergency line is blinking on

And there has been no answer on this call

Can you hear me?

In my pursuit of happiness.

<u>Rock-bottom</u>

Purification of my soul

Begins where I reach rock-bottom

On the day I look

At self-sabotage pointing a gun to my foot

When I look

And see my double evil twin

The evil twin called the enemy within

At sunset when I see

See that the warden of my prison

The prison of many regrets and sorrows is me

And I have swallowed the key to my cell

How do I set me free?

Then the obvious comes out

I have to fight

But how do I win

A war against myself?

Hold me on the slippery road

I am trying to stand up

But I am sliding all over the place

Mud covers me

Everywhere I look is wet soil

The terrain is a slope

How do I get out of here?

I want to get out

To stand on dry ground

To walk on my feet

Headed to somewhere

You showed up on time

Can you just hold me?

On this slippery slope.

Dawn came up

Dusk bade goodbye

I am still here

There is fear in my eyes

Do you not see it?

There is a war brewing in my head

But I have no weapon

No weapon to fight off this mud

You seem like a good person

Or are you a goat in lamb's clothing?

You seem like a hero to me

Maybe it's because no one

No one has passed by this slippery slope

In a million years

Whoever you are

Don't you dare let another sun set on me

Stuck on this road

The wolves come out at night

They encircle me and smell my fear

Birds of prey fly over my head

Waiting for my last breath

The road is holding on to me

Please, pull me out

And hold me on the slippery road.

<u>Mummy dearest</u>

Dedicated to all the abused children who suffered or died in need of their mother's love.

Born needy and craving of your attention

You were the giver of life

Nine months went by quickly

As we were attached to each other

There shouldn't be any love greater than this

Then why am I thirst for it?

Why am I hungry for your attention?

If you loved me, surely, I would know it

Who is this stranger you love more?

Isn't that someone else's child?

You put him and her first

You rip the clothes off my back

And give them to strangers

You shun me and yet

You salivate for other people's children

If I had an aunt like you

All my problems will be over

If you were my grandmother

I would not lack love.

I jump and I skip, you take no notice

I beg on my knees, you see me not

If I were to scream for you mummy dearest

Your ears are full of wax

If I cry for love and acceptance

You tell me to buckle up

Whatever happened to you?

When did motherhood and love became two separate entities?

You have made your motherhood a limited liability

What do I have to do for you to love me?

If you don't love me

How am I supposed to think and believe?

Believe that anyone else will?

I have been a champion bull

Yet you didn't attend the ceremony

I have been a slayer of the dragon

Yet I didn't see you praise my heroism

Oh mother!

You left me hollow and empty

The road I travel is too long

The miles too deep

You nailed me to a cross

And the arms are hurting for your embrace

Would you ever love me?

I am waiting for the day that you will pick a dial

And tell me to come home

That everything is gonna be okay

The day I can quench my thirst for mother's milk

The day I can hear you sing me a lullaby

A lullaby so sincere that I can sleep

For the first time in forever

Come close mother

You are my gate to this hellhole

Why won't you blink for an answer?

Will you ever at least try?

Try to love me for the first time

Am I not what you had in mind?

How could you be cold, so callous?

Where is your heart mummy dearest?

I need your love.

Pressed on the outside

Circle of life

The ball of living

There is a button inside

Press it and the pressure takes over

Pressure so high that you can't breathe

You want to jump towards the button

But only floating is allowed inside

How do you swim in air?

The pressure blows your mind

The anguish takes over

Like pain of being burnt alive

Terror takes over

Tears flow for a second

But the pressure

Takes even that away

You may reach the button, eventually

And that's the day you will realize

Realize that

You were being pressed on the outside.

The throne of no kingship

Dedicated to worldwide women who are suffering with infertility and can't afford any help

Her eyes have sunken the sockets

She has become as thin as a reed

There is no joy in her

It has vaporized

Her ears ache for a chance

A chance of good news

But every moon phase

The river of blood she loathes

Haunts her

It has become a monster

Taking away the life in her bones

Because year after year

There is no prince to sit on the throne.

She is an island of solitude

It never used to be like this

She was the life of the party

Once upon a time

The friends she made

Became a thorn in her backside

They all planted and harvested their pumpkins

But her field gives her no yield

How is she supposed to hang around?

Harvesters with their grand pumpkins

When her field is a desert?

The man she loves tries to console her

But she can't hear it

How can he understand her problems?

When she herself can't understand them?

Whenever hope is extended to her

She winces and braces

For how can today be better

When yesterday was denied?

Her marriage is hanging by the thread

She didn't know how much

She wanted to be the queen with a prince

Until now

When they told her she can't?

She reads and hears of children

Children who are being massacred everyday

And her uterus leaps out of her

Oh, the horror!

She will be the greatest mother

That the world has ever seen

If only she can get the chance

How dare the injustice of this place?

Why do delinquents eat the food of the masters?

Why does God deny her what she already is?

A mother without a child.

She walks like a zombie

Head down and shoulders burdened

Burdened with what she carries

She sees the windows dressed with her dream

And she can't help it but walk into the store

And let pain wash over her

Peace they didn't extend

She doesn't understand why she does this to herself

But a part of her wants to be a part of the mothers' club

That visits such stores and

Another part is just a monster

A monster that is feeding on her pain

She feels the tears running down her face

She throws the objects of her dream back down

Where she took them

And run out of the store

Running to her barrenness.

There is help but she can't afford it

It costs millions she doesn't have

There are gurus who swear by

Natural healing and she has tried it all

Her bedroom has become a clinic

She is a woman possessed

There is no sweetness in the love deed

Just methodical experiments

To see if nine months from then

Her joy could be restored

She could hold her child

Be a woman of her age

To smile and love again

All she wants is a prince

A prince for the kingship.

I have tried

Can they see me?

How invisible am I?

Have you ever swum the ocean?

Only to hear the lifeguard ask you

Ask you which fishpond you swam from?

Have you ever run a marathon?

Only to have an ant ask you

Ask you why giants' sweat for doing nothing?

Have you ever tried to love someone?

Only to be pushed out

Pushed out and end up alone?

Have you ever tried very hard?

Very hard to make a positive turnaround of your life,

Only to have people in your life remind you

Remind you constantly of what a failure you were?

Why is my trying not visible?

Only my once-in-a while mistakes

Those are magnified under the microscope.

It hurts like hell to know that all your shovelling

All your shovelling is not picking up dirt,

It hurts so bad when the bad-luck

The bad luck that has become of you,

Becomes your fault because it's you

I tried, I got knocked down

I got up million times and

I didn't get any one cheer

I am of you

How do you think it feels?

To know that all your trying

Your trying is worthless

You are but a shadow

Oh, how I have tried.

I didn't mean for them to reject me,

But they did

I didn't mean to say yes to a cartoon

But I married a jerk

I didn't mean to be a bottom-feeder

Yet I am one anyway

I have tried,

I have cried,

How do you not see the tears on my face?

How do you not feel of the brokenness?

The brokenness that my heart carries

I feel so alone and drunk of pain

Because I am invisible.

On life support

Fear is for the gutless

Rifles, bows and arrows are my utensils

Who dares question anything of me?

For I don't shoot to kill

But I know that death will find you

There was a heart on me

Some years gone by

It's been ripped out of me

It's dead

The little voice, that annoying little voice

Is on life support.

I was kind, sweet and caring once upon a time

Now revenge is my calling card

Shame is something I buried with tokens of peace

I burrow in holes, waiting for the time

Time to execute justice

Darkness encompasses me

It's a warm welcome

For the shadow that has become of me

No fear, no heart, no surrender

The conscience is on life support.

<u>**Stand up**</u>

Downtrodden, hurt and abused,

I will need stitches,

Where my heart was is now a gaping hole

Empty with nothing to fill the void

I want to sleep all day

I want to eat all day

I wish someone was there to tell me,

Tell me to stand up.

Everyone needs a cheering squad,

I fired mine

I don't know how

I don't know why and

I don't know when

All I know is that they aren't here

I miss them

I would want them to tell me

Tell me to stand up.

My life is a dense fog

There are no survivors on the peninsula

The peninsula of desperation

Oh, how I am longing for more energy to flow,

For more zeal to fire me up

So that I can shake off

The crippling sensation on my legs

So that I can stand up

Just one more time.

Don't stand there and not clap your hands

Stand up and clap for me

Stand up and give me seven cheers

Seven cheers for each day of the week

Maybe you don't understand me,

I have travelled around galaxies on my sore feet

I have been hallucinating with exhaustion

So today when I took off my bathrobe

Glossed up my lips and

Forced myself out of the cage of despair

By standing up,

You have to stand up for me

Because I am standing up for me.

<u>Wounded animal</u>

I stepped into a trap

A trap that was meant

Meant to maim me

I managed to free myself

Free myself from the razor-sharp weapon

There is excruciating pain,

Shooting up and down my paw

As I limp away

As a wounded animal.

There was a day

A day I made it into the village

I wanted a friendly face

A new master to pet me

To welcome me home

To love me

To accept me

But they were anything but welcoming

Pitch-forks were gathered

Things were thrown at me

Horrible words punched me

They told me

To never show my face again

My face in the village.

Since then I have learned

Learned not to wonder

Far and near the village

The torment they gave me

Was tattooed on my soul

The shouts

The torture made me realize

Realize that

It's always them against me.

So now I walk about

Looking for limping animals

Wounded animals like me

The ones who know the truth

The truth about the villagers

The truth about the traps

Traps set up near every food source

The truth about the trauma

The trauma that caused us to hide

To hide by putting up shields

Shields so strong

They are made of titanium

This way, we are protected.

I lash out

Because it's safer that way

I walk away

Before they do

Because I don't think my heart can take it

Take another stab to it

It has become a sieve

The stabs of yesterday

Were too deep

They didn't heal

I learned to play tortoise

A tortoise with a hard shell

A hard shell I hide into

When a threat comes closer

Even perception of it

I shut down my door

And pull the curtains

It's safer in there.

I am sensitive to air now

How can I not be?

Air caused whirlwinds

And it caused clouds to gather

Clouds that became dark

And brought torrential downpours

Downpours that didn't end

End to let me dry and

Gather myself for a different season

I am a wounded animal

My environment scares me

It's tough in the jungle.

Entombed but not buried

I am alone again

The highway keeps getting longer

The stretch of my journey too far

I want to speak but there is only air

I want to burn something for a signal

A signal to come to my rescue

Looking yonder there is a pigeon

Even it is not alone

They squawk in groups

Birds of same feathers

But I am all alone

Entombed but not buried.

The vows I took many years ago

Were broken by the snake in my grass

The fruit of my womb

Didn't germinate and it too became a tomb.

Friends have run for the hills

I have seen terrorists with vests

Vests strapped on with more friends than I do

The place I stay in,

The room I live in, is a tomb.

Dark matter on a pin

The anguished guttural cries of a child

A child who sits alone in the dark

The wandering eyes, the search

For the one whom I share a centre vault

A vault on my stomach with

Utter despair

Pain, shrill, pain

Drip, drip, drip

Beep, beep, the sounds of machines

Machines tied to a tiny stature

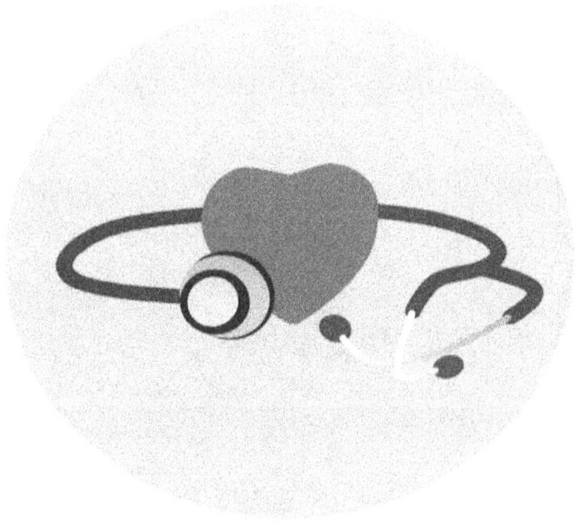

Of a child who is not supposed to know disease

The giver of life came back, stood by

Tears streaming down her face

Is that fear I see in her eyes?

The worm has rattled my little body

It was not meant to be this way

I want to go home

Grow up there,

Learn to sit, crawl, stand and walk

To carry the food box and learn

Learn playground hymns

But I am stuck here,

In a room with a single bed

Mum and I in tears

She holds me in her arms

Wants to sing a soothing lullaby

But I hear the pain of her sigh

She holds me but the pain won't go away

I want to play

Isn't that what children do?

Which road has life taken me on?

I want to go home

To see the blue skies

But no, I am stuck here

Pain, shrill, pain

Beep, beep, beep

The sound goes on

Make way for the young dearly scared

It is dark matter

Dark matter on a pin.

I am a giant

Born female,

Yet have strength of ten Adonis'

Born weak and pacified,

Yet hope holds dear

Don't let my fancy name fool you

Don't let regrets from yonder

Rob you of seeing me,

Despite all my failures

Despite all my imperfections

I am still a giant.

Bring me down all you want,

Taunt me like your life depends on it

Reject me, refuse me

Walk away, abandon me,

Come morning,

I will plump up my pillow,

Put both my feet on the ground and run,

I am gonna smile

While running because I deserve to,

There is a secret you never found out

I am more than what you made of me.

I am transparent,

I am deep

I am an onion,

There is a multitude of me underneath,

I am scared, but not terrified

I am down-trodden,

But not out

I am in this for the long-haul

There is no 'I can't' in the volume

The volume of my dictionary

There is no surrender

I will raise up my hands in dark moments

But I am not walking away

I may shed a million tears

But I will vacuum them dry.

I am taller than you see

I am stronger than you see

I am an iceberg

I am a brave warrior

The sound of my roar chases

Chases the king of the jungle

I stand tall

In the order even I can't comprehend

I hold a bazooka in one hand

And a machine-gun the other

I am a one-woman army

Don't let my glossy lips and

My made-up face fool you

Underneath is a hidden cavern of a warrior

I am a giant.

<u>I was born yesterday</u>

The promises kept coming

Things were going to get better

They would love me like

One of their own

They would accept me

Flaws, warts and all

They forgot something

I was not born yesterday.

The messages were sent

Then why did I still want to converse?

The phone rang

There was no one on the other side

The innate need of wanting to belong

Took over

I wanted to forgive everyone

To forget everything

To be a new born

As if I was born yesterday

The peace was not extended

Their love is like a tortoise head

It comes out to play when there is food

Threaten a little

And the head goes home

Then I am left standing alone.

I have tried to learn

To learn who they are

But they are a wall of thorns

That I can't climb

I am walking away

Empty and hollow

Wishing for their love

But I know they don't have it

I have been asking to borrow a shovel

From a wild warthog

Maybe if I was born yesterday

I wouldn't have a choice

But stand their empty lies

But now I go my way

Knowing I was born alone.

<u>Tears I will not wipe</u>

In foetal position,

I weep bitterly,

Room so cold,

Ashen heap where the fire used to burn,

Curtains dragged across the boxed glass

Quiet, oh so quiet,

I could hear a pin drop

But I am not listening

The high wave of the ocean within is bursting out,

I feel my liver could be washed ashore with it,

The tears are my friends now,

Wet, dreary, sad little waterfalls

These are all I have right now,

They are tears I will not wipe.

They gathered at a witch's coven,

They jeered and mocked me

I can still hear their voices in chorus

Oh, the Hades spirit of belittling

They told me what a failure they thought of me.

The cheap phone I held to my battered ears

Should have fallen to pieces on hardwood floor

But I kept holding on

Maybe I was daring the devil for a good heart?

I could taste the salt, the sour taste

Of the tears I will not wipe.

They sentenced me to a comical position,

Put a plaque of no one matters across my chest

The crime for the punishment?

I had fallen in love with a confused,

A confused, deranged, sick man

Who didn't know who he was,

But my prosecutors said I should have known

The judges of my life seem to

Get away with sentencing

Sentencing the innocent to prison

But who can stand against such tyranny?

They think they can get away with it

But will they ever?

I am waiting for justice and fairness

And until that day comes

I will not wipe my tears.

Nothing to lose

The room is empty

The sun peeps through the windows

There was a time

When everything was here

When this house was a home

A time when it all came together

But now, it's a box of concrete.

The job I had is lost

The money well is a dry pond

I have walked thither and yonder

And found no open palms

My drawers are empty

Even the cockroaches

Have found new residence

They had nothing to stay for.

The love I had blew away

I didn't know how light as a feather it was

Security of a future ripped apart

There was no remorse

I thought all my ducks were in a row

He scorched my heart

And left me holding an urn of its ashes

To blow anger

To whistle death

I walk all over

I fear nothing

What else is there to lose?

I see a stranger who is abhorrent and I say;

Walk slowly and don't jump suddenly

Talk to me like I am a person

Don't be rude just because I am a stranger

There is darkness all over me

Anger and outburst the safest places to go

I would tread carefully if I were you

Because there is nothing in this world

Nothing as dangerous as a person

A person with nothing to lose.

Justice

I bite my nails

My body is shaking

I want to shout

But words won't come out

The defendant is a drama queen

She terrorized my heart

She is cold and distant

There is no jury in this courtroom

The judge is the universe

I am the witness and the victim

How dare she?

She was supposed to love her child,

She doesn't

She was supposed to care,

She won't

She was supposed to be there

But she ran the other way

Now here we are

I want justice

I need peace

But she won't surrender

She looks from the bench of the accused

Like a justified warrior who did her job

Too bad that she may have broken some laws

But she swears she got the job done

How does she know?

Because I am alive, aren't I?

<u>Unforgiven</u>

The chains on my ankles won't break

The ones on my wrists,

I have chosen

To stare at them and twist them around

The rotten tall iron bars are

But a foot in my face

I miscalculated

I made some errors

I misjudged

And got over
to the wrong
side of the
lane

Now I am unforgiven.

The jail is a prison I will not escape

The offended made themselves the victims,

The victims, the jury and the judges

I am human too but

They are human more

I played the wrong deck of cards

Gambled with people's souls

I loved, I lied

I united with others; I fell apart

The prison wall I built myself is too thick

Because in my reality

I am unforgiven.

Tread lightly and tread softly

Don't play games with people's minds

They told me of karma

But I believed it was a bad joke

I listened to a preacher preach

Preach about laws of the universe

I giggled as my parachute was flying

Flying higher than the universe

But it happened

It nose-dived

I fell head first on a concrete

To end up unforgiven.

What do you see?

What do you see when you look at me?

Do you see my beauty?

What do you think about my weight?

Am I short or tall?

If you look

You will see the outside

But if you choose to see

Really see me

What would you see?

I am a pot of boiling water

There is steam coming out of my ears

Touch me and I will burn you

I wasn't born this way

But the boiling water gives me comfort

Comfort to know that

Come tomorrow

There will be a fresh brew of tea

For today, just look.

There is a storm that wants to burst

To burst out of me

Life has gone too far

What fresh hell is on the horizon?

Should I hiss a thunder?

Or launch a field of lightning

To this darkness?

It's all too much drama

You all want a piece of me

But I just want peace

You drag me to hell and

Forget that I am not made for it

Please don't

Just don't

No matter whatever you want to see

I am still just me

Look and look again

Just make sure

Make sure that you see me.

The world I live in

It's a wonderful world isn't it?

Well some of the times,

For the other times,

I am not so sure

I have seen evil people prosper,

And good people suffer

I have seen ant-soldiers eating gravel,

Yet I have seen sloths sitting

Sitting on the most-high branch

Branch of an oak tree

How did they get there?

The world I live in is smoke and mirrors

It's a gamble,

It's a game,

There is only one rule to the game

Play yourself silly

You are born, then what?

What is next and according to whom?

For most,

The pre-game match is set in a prison cell

A cell for a life sentence

The warden swallowed the key

And transferred the whole block to the Hades

The match is fixed,

The referees follow the rules of the Master

But who is the Master?

Do we choose what happens?

Or does life choose for us?

The world I live in is corrupt and evil

I wonder what is the point to any

Any and all of this?

Is there a just reward for anybody?

The bad-asses are our leaders

No, there is no room for error

Good people can't lead,

They don't know how

History teaches us nothing

What's life, eh, if we don't make it harder on ourselves?

We have to make ourselves feel like we earned it

Seriously, we got this

Wouldn't you agree?

That it's a wonderful life?

Good mothers don't bear children

Bad mothers,

The ones who are kookier than a cannabis pot,

Yes, they will bear a dozen

Good trees don't bear fruit

The fruits of the divine are sacred

And the snake from the garden decides who eats

We applaud stupid,

Intelligence is not cool

I am part of this crossword puzzle

Crossword puzzle called life

Only thing is I don't know, "You are screwed across"

So, I am waiting for the next hint

Isn't it a wonderful life?

<u>Peace they didn't extend</u>

I looked back

Maybe I shouldn't have

But I did

Deep regret was gnawing my heart

I knew then what I had to do

There was no next village

If the one behind me was burning.

I crossed the river full of crocodiles

I climbed the mountain with a steep terrain

No trees to hold on to

I walked through the forest in which I fought bears

There were wasps and gnats

Clinging to my skin

But I soldiered on.

I saw the smoke from afar

Reached the village and saw the burnt landscape

I looked for survivors

And saw the anger on their faces

The match-stick that had started the fire

The match-stick was mine

I extended my hand

But they didn't shake it

I signalled the hand gesture for peace,

They didn't see it

I waved the white flag on the tallest mountain

They didn't look

They rejected my peace.

There is a river on top of the mountain

When they see me

They see a broken woman

A woman incapable of friendships

They reached out

And I lashed out

Like a wounded animal

Now all they see is a crazy lady

A loner

No, better yet

An insufferable loner.

When they stare at me

They see a beautiful woman

They see a woman

Who should be in a happy,

A happy, romantic relationship

I tell them I am not looking

The whole room boos me

How dare I?

They ask

A beautiful woman is to be shared

To be shared to as many

Many love conquests as possible

They see a selfish queen bee

Who doesn't want bees to rest,

To rest in her blossomed flower.

When they pass me by,

They can't remember my face

My name is a foreign language

I wanted to ask

To ask for directions

But how dare I?

The road ahead is to be found alone

Anyone who asks for directions

Is cheating

A pedestrian is not to be afraid

Afraid of hidden bushes

Bushes hide little creatures

Creatures of life's forces.

When they look at me

As l ask for money

Beg for a job

They see a lazy woman

An unqualified delinquent

I am supposed to walk this world

Walk this world with arms deep

Deep in hard manual labour

Anything else is deemed too good

Too good for the likes of me

If I come back and put up a tent

A tent of a beggar

They send their hounds to chase me away

Whatever they see of me

I want them to remember

To remember that they don't see all of it

There is so much I would love to tell them

There are so many reasons

I do what I do

If they were willing to listen

I would tell them

Then they would know

That even though

I look brown like a desert

Swim against the currents

And climb trees of thorns

There is a river on top of the mountain.

I wouldn't have known

If you told me that life is not easy

If you told me that people hurt others

If you told me family is overrated

If you told me that school

School is an exercise to servanthood

I would have scoffed and run away

Because I wouldn't have known.

If you told me

Told me that success is not guaranteed

If you had said that the man,

The man I was marrying

Was a deranged lunatic

If you even set me down

Crystal ball in the centre

And gathered

Gathered all the magic of earth

To show me that I would be here

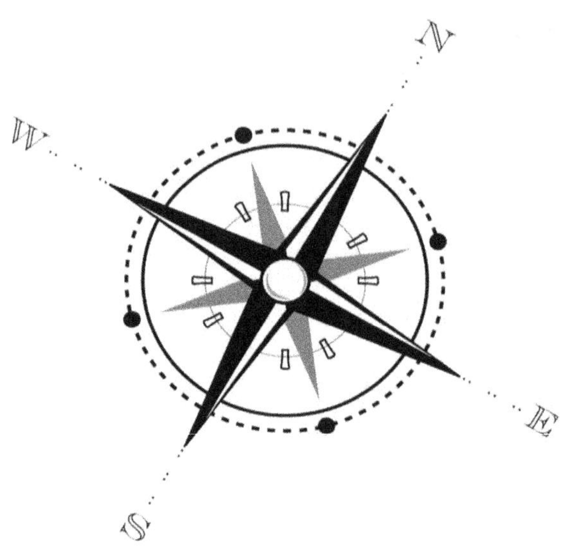

Here at a crossroads

Pain to the North

Lonely to the South

Broke and broken at the East

And misery to the West

Not sure which compass route to take?

I would have shaken my head

I wouldn't have known.

Run on your elbows

I was one of them

They singled me out

Then they sat me on a throne

A throne reserved for a criminal

Charges were read

And I was condemned

Condemned to run on my elbows.

I couldn't go far

I didn't know how to hide

To hide from people who look like me

Like me from afar

The punishment was harsh

The sentence brutal

I was to dig through

Dig through the Sahara Desert

For a fruit

They gave me a lemon

For food

They said there are

Crawling creatures

Crawling creatures to catch in the desert

The crime I was being accused of

I was being accused of falling in love

The boy had lied

He had broken the queen

Queen of the universe's heart

He was the one who had gotten away

But the guillotine was mine

It was for the gullible

The hanging was scheduled

Drama was needed

And I was cast into play

An unwilling fugitive

For the evil wickedness

Of soft evil faces

It was a school

But they had turned it into

A school of sharks

Those were not children

They were children possessed

Possessed to torment

Torment and torture the innocent

Now they search for me

Nah, no, no, no

Stay far away from me

Don't ever find me

After you made me

Made me run on my elbows.

Just one more time

I am caught up in the mundane details of life,

I got up yesterday, the day before and today,

I am up this morning,

Terror stricken,

The shadow that is me,

I am afraid of my life,

I want to hide

But there is nowhere to hide,

I have to keep moving,

So maybe,

If I try today,

Just one more time.

Thunderclaps, bolt lightning,

The stage is set, lighting, microphone,

The costume I am adorned into,

 I have to perform,

I signed on with the universe talent agent,

Sometimes I am winging it,

The drama called life continues,

Even if I want to press pause,

There is no pause,

I have to keep acting.

The applause I hear,

The clapping I relish,

Sometimes there is dead silence,

I can hear the crickets chirping,

Because the performance didn't deliver,

The audience are here to judge,

Do they know, how hard I am trying?

I am holding on to hope,

My hope is made of glass,

I am tired,

I am exhausted,

Yet I can't fold the cards on my table,

I have to keep playing,

The joker is of a poker face,

I don't know what tomorrow is going to bring,

So maybe if I try,

Just one more time.

I am on the lane of marathon,

Yet I want to sprint,

Running to nowhere,

End of road ahead,

Brakes I pushed too hard

Are starting to wear thin,

Will I make it over the fast-approaching bend?

I don't know what is on the other side,

But there is no stopping now,

I have to keep moving,

I have to try,

Just one more time.

I pull myself by the bootstraps,

The calf of my leg is tense,

I am climbing a high mountain,

The path is winded,

The summit so close,

Yet so far from my grasp,

But maybe if I try,

Just one more time.

Closet without door

I just want the sun to shine through

To give light inside the eye of a hurricane

It's been too dark

The blackness so thick that I can touch it

Bred to suffocate in the canyons of Mars

No soul comes to rescue

Even the rabbits have burrowed deeper

The eagles fly higher

The bird nests are tightened to branches

Walk alone, on the peninsula of destitute

The destination is there somewhere

They tell me

But when I get there won't demons with pitch-forks

Be waiting for me?

I keep walking

But I don't want another hell

The one I have lived is more than enough

The drought came to stay

The roof of my house was iron brass

And the soil was cement

Drink and eat

Make merry they said

How do I show them the prison I am in?

It seems to hold one and I am in it

It is a closet without a door.

<u>Fire burning in my life</u>

The raging inferno

Has been encouraged

The fires that were trying to burn down

Are now consuming my very soul

I wanted to walk out

But the door burnt first

I wanted to leave without any burn marks

But I am not so sure anymore.

The water was poured on me

All it did was leave me drenched

Wet, soggy but still burning

The powder from the pressure can

Was sprayed on me

It hit me with the speed of its velocity

All it did was make me

Make me look like a ghost

A person full of ash.

No one seems to know

Know how to stop the raging inferno

I am burning up

And I want the burning sensation

And the hot rigid air to stop

To stop forever

So that there won't be any fire left

Any fire left burning in my life.

In the dead of the night

My garden of Eden became a warzone,

Horror stories as the crib I had known

Became a violent tunnel of raging waves

Water was leaving my pool

I was a water animal

I couldn't breathe

It became blindingly dark

Then suddenly I was being banished

The comforts of my first home were out of reach

Being forced down a tunnel

It was slippery,

So down the slope I went

The tunnel suddenly became bottle-necked

It was a tough place to move

In the dead of the night.

I had to force myself down the tunnel

Little pool water surrounded me

I needed that water like a fish in the deep

Then piercing noises of beeping machines

People shouting and screaming

I was evacuated from the best

Best home in the world

That home was dark but I could see

The rent was free

Food came on demand,

Drinks were a gallon per ten

Comforting and plush it was

But into an open space I came

A darker world in my opinion

But my old home couldn't accommodate

Accommodate my growth spurt

All this horror happened

In the dead of the night.

<u>Holding on</u>

I don't know why

I am still holding on

Knives and machetes have slashed my flesh

To carve deep tattoos

Tattoos not for an exchange for a dollar

But tattoos to show where I have been

Tears have been my friends

They jeer and they mock

They lay down and throw away

The injustice alone

Is enough to make your insides churn

I see it, I cry, I laugh

Laughter is better

To counter the evil

I have nowhere to hide

So, I will stand firm

Because for all that life

Life has thrown at me

I am still holding on.

Live under a bridge or

Live in a mansion

Healthy as a fiddle or

Sick as a madman

Married, single or confused

Who dares tell me that life is not worthy living?

Because no matter what life spits at me

I will still be holding on.

Draw the sword

Life so deep, so dark

The terrain so vast and

Winter snow covers the expanse

Tall limbs of dried trees

In a forest with no game

Breathe frost breath

Cover your head and your body

The boots you walk in

Will not last the race

But the race will not be stopped

There will be a shoe shop on the way

The gun rang and everyone is racing.

No one knows the finish line

Nobody has discovered the secret yet;

You can run,

You can stop

Are you sitting or swimming?

Anything goes

But the game is still played

No one gets out of the race

Until they reach the finish line

The finish line is different for each athlete

Some get it after a short distance

And others have to run a marathon

There are few cheerers on the side tracks

The referees are unknown

But you will hear their whistle once in a while

You can follow the whistle command or

Keep doing whatever you were doing before

I swear,

No one is going to stop you.

If you go on this race without warming up,

You may still make it

But the ones that are dressed for the weather

The ones who cheat once in a while

And the lucky ones who know the laws and rules

The laws that were supposed to be handed

Handed to every athlete but weren't

Those are the ones who will win

The winning can be achieved during the race

Should you reach your end of the line

Your fellow competitors will gather

Gather and talk of a great game you played

Most of their talk will be lies

To make other athletes feel better

Don't struggle,

Don't fret

Stand up tall

For in this race

No one gets out alive

Draw your sword and learn to win.

<u>Blackhole</u>

Rotten to the core he was

A slime ball bundled into a rag of flesh

Despicable, wicked little man

The man who dared torture a child

A child who just lost her father

Dark, swirling of life he sent me to.

Father was buried under a tree

Cycle of moon ago

They came as if to show mercy

Crocodile tears on their faces

And told of how a different environment would do me good

If only I knew how to fight

But I was a child

That man touched me where he wasn't supposed to

I carry the scars of broken innocence

I will walk around with tears on my face

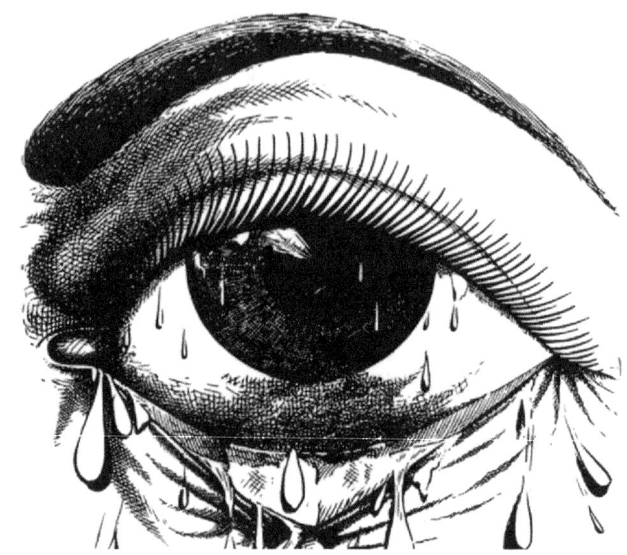

Looking for a way out of this blackhole.

Losing a father was tragic enough

But being abused in the same quarter takes the punch

I was an orphan

A grieving child looking for solace

But that slimeball chose to do evil

These are tears I will not wipe

The scars that pair with the tears are transparent

They go right through me

Will I ever get out of this blackhole?

The mirror that screams

Tears all over my pillow

My eyelids are pumped and puffed

I wake up,

Holding on to the walls

Legs wobbly like a little lamb's

I want to climb back into bed

But I have to keep going

There is darkness in my room

And in my soul

I should light a wicker stick

But I don't want to see

If I look in the mirror

Who will be looking back at me?

Is there any light left in the darkness?

What is this animal within?

The animal that makes me

Make me understand

Even the wickedest of them all

It is scaring me

How do I understand?

They say he killed, I get it

She stole, well I have thought about it

She is crazy, well me too

He is this or that and I am too

So, I know if I look

The animal will jump out

The mirror will scream.

Glass eyelids

From a distance,

It's a speck of dust,

Up close, it's an angel,

I see you,

I hear you

I want to say my soul is yours

I see right through you,

I am made for this and that,

Deep within,

I hear the screams your soul sings,

I see the shattered pieces

Where your heart used to be,

I see behind the façade,

Through your glass eyelids.

Layered up to the hilt,

The shimmer of hurt and anger,

I feel it,

The wrestling match,

Between the bitterness and love,

You are trying ever so hard,

You are climbing

The highest peak without oxygen,

But there is nowhere to hide,

I see you.

Twisted but not broken,

You stand up tall,

Yet you are a dwarf inside,

You have a job but no work,

Yet you are holding on,

Tightening the grip

The mist of a ghost night,

The penetrating sunrise

A glorious sight for a welcoming tomorrow,

You don't want to fight,

You don't want to stand still,

The curiosity of a cat that overrides

Overrides your common senses,

You will not wear your heart on the sleeve,

You will protect it in a titanium cage,

Is it fright or fight?

You have no cave to run to

I see you

Really see you.

<u>**Just fine**</u>

When you walk into their lives

If they choose to make peace

Or they choose to start a war

Just remember whatever happens

You will be just fine.

When they tell you, you are worthless?

When they use you and discard you?

They will tell you they are better

They may even make you think

That you can't make it without them

But you my dear have a secret

Whisper it to yourself

'I will be just fine'.

Life is not theirs to give

They can manipulate but they can't win

They can choose to stay or to go

To love you or to hate you

Either way my friend

You will be just fine.

Racism and Africa

Different colours of mud

Children of men come in different colours

Some dark, some light

The difference is so small

Yet, there are different little wars fought everywhere,

You better learn to fight or you will lose

Every-day you walk out of your door

Check if your stamina is in full supply

Then go and fight,

Fight other children of men

Because you are a different colour of mud.

You might get bullied for it

Some have died because of it

They will break your heart for it

They will look down on you because of it

When they discriminate against you and

Remember this, they will

Stand up and fight back

Because you didn't do anything wrong

You are just a different colour of mud.

You might have to try ten times harder to get there

Because you are different

You might have to get educated twenty times more

But you will always be uneducated

Hush now my dear

You are fine the way you are

You are great in ways they don't want to find out

Worry not my beloved,

The name of the game is racism

I don't know where you apply for colour

But if I did know, I would apply to be a chameleon

To have all the colours so that I can fit in everywhere

But alas, I am me

A different colour of mud.

Same flesh, same blood but different outer-shells

It will cause rivalry

Sneaky games are played because of it

Which team are you playing for?

Are there any real winners?

Or we all ought to be ashamed of ourselves?

It is just paint differences

Different colours of houses

Yes, your body is a house for your mind, heart and spirit.

Some houses may be mansions, huts, detached or apartments

But still made of same brick and mortar

All the sad, pathetic Earth games

Before we all sleep forever

Funny don't you think?

Yet so painful

Because of different colours of mud.

Cure mother continent

Mother continent is sick,

The chronic disease has been terminal for centuries,

She keeps going on hind broken legs

It's time a cure was found for mother continent.

The disease is poverty inducing, civil war causing,

Foolish politics partaking, economy shrinking,

It is a never-ending cycle of pain,

Anguish of disorganization,

Soul-crushing winds of desert,

Help me to heal mother continent.

It started with selling each other

To foreigners for a quick buck,

Now we have become slaves to the same foreigners,

Only difference is this time

We put ourselves in containers,

To go get bottom of pit jobs,

That their own bottom-feeders don't want,

How long should we be slaves in cold,

Northern regions of the world?

Barren lands with hardly any rich minerals that my mother carries?

I see them my brothers and sisters,

Educated at home but not enough for faraway

Forced to take de-meaning, soul-crushing jobs

Because there is nowhere to hide

Ah, my people,

Isn't it time we healed mother continent?

Because everyone is trying to survive,

The discord to life is over-limit

People hassle, open little stalls to sell,

Stand on dark corners of the dust-roads,

Overcharging their neighbour

Because they don't know

When the next customer will be,

Politicians act the exact same way

And steal from their own,

Schools are barely open,

Knowledge is questionable,

Hospitals are like God's waiting room,

Dysfunction is high

There is too much bad in mother continent,

When is it going to end?

This feels like we are cattle going for the dip,

Mass numbers to a different kind of pain,

Where do we run off to?

Sometimes I wonder what life

Life for a child born in mother continent is all about?

Are they indeed born to suffer?

Mother continent is sick and bruised,

But the power of change is in our hands

Do we leave mother continent to die?

Or do we all unite and say enough is enough?

We can work together towards a common goal,

The goal to heal mother continent.

Will you hold my hand?

Stand with me and let's rebuild?

We are capable of more than we think,

We can turn the life of Africa around,

For our future and

For generations to come after us

Let's cure mother continent.

<u>**Now I know**</u>

Everyone is ever so nice, they said

No one cares about your outwards look, they lied

The world judges me

They hold my integrity, uniqueness and heart for ransom

Someone ought to pay them

They are owed because I walk among them

They are owed because even if I bleed red

They decided theirs is the only real blood

Sit with us, live among us, laugh with us

Look in their reflection in the water well as they say this

And you will see their sinister eyes cause waves at you

As for me, myself and I

Now I know.

They call me a demon, even the ones with hearts of stone

They call me a thief, though I have yet to steal from them

They call me an ape, a sub-human

Even though I am wonderfully and fearfully made

They call me a lazy and an angry woman

But they forget the lower pay they offered

The snide little comments they passed unto me at the
water cooler

They forget to tell me job well done for job well done

They don't remember the promotion they overlooked
me for.

They all forget the prejudice that they write, sing and
parade

Of what they call my ugliness

They push me down, shove me over

And if I answer back

Then what they thought of me all along is confirmed

It's a game they rigged against me and my kind

I am damned if I do and I am damned if I don't.

For every trailer trash

If it doesn't look like me,

They are disappointed

If one of my brothers or sisters break a rule,

They sit on their fat behinds

Smug, evil faces, smirking to the sound

The warrior screams of a keyboard soldier

With a vendetta to paint all my family dark and evil

They think I don't know but now I know.

If their kind breaks a law, it's madness

If mine does, that's who we are

They tell me to stand up for myself

But I know that they don't mean that

Why do I have to prove myself a hundred times?

Hundred times more than a flea bag of different colour?

They want me to see them as human

Even when they deny me mine

Who are they lying to?

I have eyes and I see it

And now I know the ugly truth.

Africa, my sorrow

Whatever happened to you?

You are the first-born

You hold in you the most stable land mass there is

There are few and far in-between hurricanes

The volcanos stopped for you equators ago

Earthquakes are not your portion,

So beautiful,

Sunsets that will melt the hardest of hearts

The weather regions

That are as warm as the kiss of the sun

Extreme winters is a fiction story to you

Blessed mother-nature

Oh, womb of humanity, why?

The cradle for mankind they called it,

The civilizations that were unmatched,

Egypt was on the far corner,

Diamond mines were pocketed in the deep south

Minerals, oil, soil that is as fertile as the valley of the Niles,

Trees that grow as tall as timber and as round as baobabs,

You lack nothing, yet you are the poorest

Oh Africa, my sorrow.

You have all kinds of animals

Do I mean on two legs or four?

Would it matter, my beloved?

Blessed abundantly you are

Yet you smell of a curse

A curse so vile,

It smells like the burning carcasses of the animals on your door-step

The animals you have let down

The animals you have sold to distant arid places

Whatever happened to those profits?

Oh Africa, you are my sorrow.

You are the richest of them all,

You are the warmest of them all,

You are the most diverse of them all,

You are the first born

Yet, you look about to ask for help

Your help comes from those coming from afar

To hand over to you what's in your backyard

Oh Africa, my sorrow.

How many centuries have to go by before you stand up for yourself?

How much minerals do they have to take from you before you wake up?

How many children must die of starvation before you realize?

Realize that your soil is the richest, it has abundance in it

How much bloodshed should you spill before you can hear the cries?

The cries of orphaned children whose father died in yet another civil war?

How much charity is enough before you pull yourself by the bootstrap?

You are a charity case

You are a basket case

My sorrow, Africa.

You are blessed, yet you don't see it,

Why do you have enough AK-47 to run down the continent?

Yet, the same soldiers are wearing dollar slippers on their feet

Why do you have all these minerals?

Minerals that should make you the envy of many?

Yet, you hand them over on free-will to the highest bidder

Well, highest bidder for a penny.

Why do your politicians seem to be from the same thread?

Victim-minded, selfish, cruel and greedy,

Yes, you were victimized, is it not over yet?

Selfish, narcissistic, men of no valour

One after another,

They all promise of change, I have yet to see it

They amass wealth that would make King Solomon jealousy

They dig deep burrows and hide it all in plain sight

They rule with an iron fist made of pebble

It's 'me, myself and I' mentality

Generation after generation

Why do we choose that which defeats us?

Oh Africa, my sorrow.

When you see the malnourished children

When you hear of the new diseases

And of the new dictator on the block

When you hear of yet another civil war

Child soldiers terrorizing huts made of mud

When you read of everyday financial meltdown

You might be forced to believe that you have nothing going for you

Yet that's not true at all

You have it all

Everything you need, but you can't seem to hold it together

Isn't it time to grow-up and mature now?

Or you want to hold on to this victim mentality forever? Rise Africa, Rise.

About the author

Acknella Ndoro is a poet and an author. She has been through some hard times including losing a parent to suicide, abuse, bullying and divorce. She writes poetry and it is like a therapy for her. This book is her debut poetry book and it shows all the sad, dark, heartfelt emotions that she has had to deal with as she went through some of the most sad, traumatic events of her life. Acknella has a diploma in Business Accounting but loves to write. She lives in Toronto, Canada.